Permission to Say No:

Empowering Yourself through Boundaries

By

Garrett Couch

First Edition

Couch, Garrett, author.

Permission to Say No: Empowering Yourself through Boundaries

Description: First Edition.

Subjects: LCSH Self-actualization (Psychology) | Personal Development. | Self-help Techniques.

First Printing, 2024

Dedication

To my dearest wife,

In every word I write and every boundary I explore, I find reflections of the love, strength, and wisdom you've shared with me. This book, while a journey through the pages of personal growth and empowerment, is imbued with the essence of the support and inspiration you've generously provided. Your unwavering belief in my endeavors and your profound understanding of the importance of saying no, to make room for what truly matters, have been my guiding light.

Thank you for being my partner in every sense of the word, for the countless moments you've said yes to us, and for teaching me the invaluable power of no. This book is a testament to our journey together and a celebration of the incredible woman you are.

With all my love and gratitude,

Garrett Couch

Preface

In a world that often praises the tireless giver and the ever-accommodating soul, the art of setting boundaries remains a nuanced path less trodden. "Permission to Say No: Empowering Yourself through Boundaries" was born from a personal journey—one that many of us embark on but few dare to speak openly about. It is a narrative woven from countless conversations, introspective nights, and the universal quest for balance and self-respect. This book is not just a guide; it is an invitation to embark on a transformative journey towards self-empowerment and genuine fulfillment.

My journey into the realm of boundaries began not with a sudden epiphany but as a gradual awakening to the realization that my constant 'yes' was not a badge of honor but a shackle limiting my potential. Like many, I was ensnared in the belief that saying yes was synonymous with being kind, helpful, and, above all, necessary to be liked and respected. It was a lesson learned in the trenches of personal experience, where the cost of non-boundaries came dressed in fatigue, resentment, and the erosion of self-identity.

The catalyst for change was as unremarkable as it was profound—a simple 'no' that felt like a daring act of rebellion. The sky didn't fall, and the earth didn't swallow me whole. Instead, I discovered space—space to breathe, think, and be. It was the first step on a path towards reclaiming my life, a step towards understanding that boundaries are not walls but bridges towards deeper connections and a more authentic existence.

This book is distilled from years of research, conversations with psychologists, and interviews with individuals from various walks of life who have navigated the treacherous waters of setting boundaries. It draws from the well of wisdom that history, psychology, and personal experience generously offer, providing a comprehensive guide to understanding, establishing, and maintaining healthy boundaries.

Chapter 1 lays the foundation, dissecting the concept of boundaries to its core. It challenges societal misconceptions and shines a light on the psychological underpinnings of why setting boundaries is inherently challenging, particularly for women. This chapter is an exploration of the landscape before us, the terrain we must navigate to understand the full spectrum of boundaries—emotional, physical, time, and energy.

In **Chapter 2**, we delve into the consequences of perpetual acquiescence—the silent toll it takes on our health, relationships, and sense of self. Through real-life anecdotes and psychological insights, this chapter aims to illuminate the often invisible cost of always saying yes and the transformative power of reclaiming our right to say no.

Chapter 3 celebrates the power of no, a simple yet revolutionary act of self-preservation and respect. It examines the societal backlash often faced by assertive women and offers strategies to stand firm in one's truth amidst the pushback. This chapter is a testament to the strength found in vulnerability and the courage required to prioritize oneself.

As we progress to **Chapter 4**, the focus shifts to practical applications—identifying personal boundaries and recognizing when they are being tested. This chapter is a toolkit, complete with exercises and reflections designed to guide the reader in a deeply personal audit of their boundaries, setting the stage for effective communication and enforcement.

Chapters 5 through 8 are dedicated to applying these principles across the spectrum of our lives—in personal relationships, the workplace, and the digital world. Each chapter is tailored to address the unique challenges and opportunities present in these arenas, offering strategies, language, and case studies to navigate them with grace and confidence.

The journey culminates in **Chapters 9 and 10**, where setting boundaries is celebrated as an act of self-care and a commitment to ongoing growth. These chapters acknowledge the challenges and setbacks inherent in boundary setting and offer wisdom on maintaining these boundaries without succumbing to isolation or burnout.

"Permission to Say No" is more than a manual; it is a manifesto for anyone who has ever felt overwhelmed, undervalued, or invisible. It is for the woman who juggles roles with grace but at the cost of her peace. It is for the professional who excels in their career but struggles to find time for self. It is for the individual who seeks to navigate the complexities of modern relationships with integrity and authenticity.

This book is a tribute to the silent strength of those who dare to say no, to those who understand that true empowerment lies in respecting oneself enough to set boundaries and demand they be honored. It is an ode to the transformative power of embracing our limits, not as constraints but as the truest expression of our self-worth and dignity.

As you turn these pages, I invite you to join me on this journey— a journey towards understanding, acceptance, and ultimately, empowerment. Let us explore together the art of saying no, not as an end but as a beginning. A beginning of a life lived on our terms, a life where our needs, desires, and well-being are not just considered but prioritized. Welcome to "Permission to Say No."

Table of Contents

Introduction 1

Chapter 1: Understanding Boundaries 5

Chapter 2: The Cost of Always Saying Yes 9

Chapter 3: The Power of No... 12

Chapter 4: Identifying Your Boundaries 15

Chapter 5: Communicating Your Boundaries....................... 19

Chapter 6: Setting Boundaries in Personal Relationships 22

Chapter 7: Setting Boundaries at Work 27

Chapter 8: Digital Boundaries.. 30

Chapter 9: The Self-Care Connection.................................. 33

Chapter 10: Overcoming Challenges 37

Conclusion: Embracing a Boundary-Minded Life 40

About the Author 44

Introduction

In the gentle unfolding of our lives, amidst the clamor of duties, expectations, and the relentless pursuit of success, there lies a subtle truth often overshadowed by the myriad demands placed upon us. It is the profound power of a simple word: "No." This book, **"Permission to Say No: Empowering Yourself through Boundaries,"** is an invitation to embark on a transformative journey towards self-awareness, empowerment, and the reclaiming of your own narrative through the deliberate setting of boundaries. It is a guide, a companion, and a reflection on the importance of asserting our right to prioritize our needs, desires, and well-being.

The genesis of this book was neither an epiphany nor a sudden burst of insight but a slow dawning realization born from years of overextension, exhaustion, and the erosion of my sense of self. Like so many, I found myself ensnared in the societal glorification of the 'yes'—a seemingly innocuous word that promised acceptance, appreciation, and the fulfillment of my roles as a professional, partner, and friend. Yet, in this incessant quest to be everything to everyone, I discovered that I had inadvertently marginalized my most critical role: being true to myself.

The journey to reclaiming my space and peace began with the recognition that setting boundaries is not an act of selfishness but one of self-respect. It is a declaration that our time, energy, and emotional well-being are precious resources not to be squandered. This book draws upon this personal journey, augmented by the collective wisdom of psychological research, interviews, and the shared experiences of those who have navigated the complex terrain of boundary setting. It is a testament to the transformative power of saying no—a power that enables us to say yes to what truly matters.

As we step into the pages of this book, we explore the multifaceted nature of boundaries. From the personal to the professional, the physical to the emotional, each chapter is designed to guide you through understanding, establishing, and maintaining the boundaries that are right for you. This exploration is not merely an academic exercise but a practical guide infused with real-life examples, exercises, and strategies tailored to empower you in the art of boundary setting.

The need for this book has never been more pressing. In an era where the lines between work and home, public and private, are increasingly blurred, the art of setting boundaries has become an essential skill for managing our lives. For women, in particular, the challenge is compounded by societal expectations that laud selflessness and sacrifice as virtues, often at the expense of personal autonomy and happiness. This book seeks to challenge these narratives, offering a new paradigm in which saying no is not just acceptable but necessary for our growth and well-being.

Chapter 1 lays the groundwork by demystifying boundaries, exploring their importance, and addressing the challenges unique to women in establishing them. It sets the stage for a deeper exploration of the consequences of living without boundaries, as discussed in **Chapter 2**. Here, we confront the toll that perpetual acquiescence takes on our lives, laying bare the hidden costs of always saying yes.

As we progress, **Chapter 3** reveals the power of no, illustrating how this simple act can transform our relationships with others and, most importantly, with ourselves. This power is not without its challenges, however. In **Chapters 4 and 5**, we delve into the practical aspects of identifying and communicating your boundaries, offering tools and language to navigate these conversations with confidence.

The heart of the book, **Chapters 6 through 8**, addresses the application of boundaries across the diverse landscapes of our lives—from personal relationships to the workplace and the digital world. Each chapter is crafted to provide you with the knowledge and strategies to manage these spaces effectively, ensuring that your boundaries are respected and maintained.

Yet, setting boundaries is not a one-time act but a continuous process of negotiation and reaffirmation. In **Chapters 9 and 10**, we explore the connection between boundaries and self-care and the challenges of upholding your boundaries in the face of resistance. These chapters are designed to reinforce the importance of persistence, self-compassion, and the ongoing practice of boundary setting.

As we embark on this journey together, it is my hope that this book will serve as more than just a guide. Let it be a catalyst for reflection, a source of inspiration, and a beacon of support as you navigate the complex but rewarding process of setting boundaries. By giving yourself the permission to say no, you are taking a powerful step towards living a more authentic, balanced, and fulfilling life.

Welcome to "Permission to Say No: Empowering Yourself through Boundaries." This is not just the beginning of a book but the start of a journey—a journey towards embracing the fullness of your potential, one boundary at a time.

Chapter 1:
Understanding Boundaries

At the heart of every meaningful interaction and personal endeavor lies the concept of boundaries. Boundaries, in their essence, are the invisible lines we draw around ourselves to protect our well-being, maintain our sense of self, and navigate our relationships with others. They are the definitions of what is acceptable and what is not, what we are willing to tolerate, and where we draw the line. In this chapter, we delve into the fundamentals of boundaries—what they are, the different types they encompass, and the unique challenges women face in establishing and maintaining them.

The Nature of Boundaries

Boundaries are, fundamentally, a form of communication. They are a way of expressing our needs, values, and limits to ourselves and to others. However, the concept of boundaries goes beyond mere communication. It is about self-awareness, respect, and the mutual understanding that for healthy interactions to occur, everyone's limits must be acknowledged and honored.

Boundaries can be categorized into several types, including emotional, physical, time, energy, and intellectual boundaries. Emotional boundaries relate to our feelings and how we manage emotional exchanges with others. Physical boundaries pertain to personal space and physical touch. Time boundaries are about how we allocate our time between various commitments and personal downtime. Energy boundaries involve managing our energy levels and deciding what we have the capacity to take on.

Intellectual boundaries concern our thoughts and ideas and the respect for diverse viewpoints.

Each type of boundary serves a distinct purpose and is integral to our overall well-being. They help us navigate our daily interactions, protect our sense of self, and maintain our integrity in various situations.

The Importance of Boundaries

Boundaries are essential for several reasons. They enable us to safeguard our well-being by preventing burnout and resentment. By clearly communicating our limits, we teach others how to treat us, thereby fostering relationships built on respect and mutual understanding. Boundaries also enhance our self-esteem and independence, as they empower us to make decisions based on our needs and values.

Furthermore, boundaries are crucial for emotional health. They allow us to separate our feelings from those of others, helping us to avoid emotional enmeshment and maintain a sense of individuality. This separation is essential for personal growth and emotional resilience, as it enables us to face life's challenges with a clear sense of who we are and what we stand for.

Women and Boundaries

For women, the challenge of setting and maintaining boundaries is often compounded by societal expectations and gender roles. Historically, women have been conditioned to be caretakers, nurturers, and pleasers—roles that emphasize the importance of others' needs over their own. This conditioning can make it difficult for women to assert their boundaries without feeling guilty or selfish.

Moreover, women often face backlash for setting boundaries, labeled as difficult, selfish, or overly sensitive. This societal pressure can deter women from asserting their limits, leading to a cycle of overextension and dissatisfaction. The struggle to set boundaries is not just a personal challenge but a reflection of broader societal dynamics that undervalue women's autonomy and well-being.

Overcoming Challenges

Establishing boundaries requires courage, self-awareness, and persistence. It begins with understanding one's own needs and values and recognizing the right to prioritize these. It also involves developing the skills to communicate these boundaries clearly and effectively, without apology.

For women, in particular, it may also require challenging internalized beliefs about self-worth and the need to please others. Overcoming these challenges involves a process of unlearning and relearning—a journey toward embracing one's right to say no and to prioritize personal well-being.

Conclusion

Understanding boundaries is the first step toward empowering oneself to establish and maintain them. This chapter has laid the groundwork by exploring the nature of boundaries, their importance, and the unique challenges faced by women in asserting them. As we move forward, we will delve deeper into the practical aspects of setting boundaries, offering strategies, tools, and insights to help you navigate this essential aspect of personal growth and well-being.

Boundaries are not just about saying no; they are about saying yes to a life of respect, integrity, and authenticity. They are the foundation upon which healthy relationships, self-respect, and personal fulfillment are built. As we embark on this journey together, let us embrace the power of boundaries to transform our lives and the world around us.

Chapter 2:
The Cost of Always Saying Yes

In the tapestry of human interaction, the threads of yeses weave a complex pattern of connections, commitments, and obligations. While saying yes can open doors to new opportunities and nurture relationships, an unchecked habit of always agreeing can exact a heavy toll on our personal well-being, relationships, and sense of self. This chapter delves into the multifaceted cost of always saying yes, exploring its impact on our lives and underscoring the crucial need for setting boundaries.

The Burden of Overcommitment

At first glance, saying yes seems like the key to being a dedicated friend, a reliable family member, and an invaluable employee. However, this seemingly benign affirmation can lead to overcommitment—a state where the demands on our time, energy, and emotional resources far exceed our capacity to meet them. Overcommitment not only strains our mental and physical health but also diminishes the quality of our contributions and our satisfaction in roles we otherwise value and enjoy.

The physical toll is undeniable, manifesting in symptoms of stress, sleep disturbances, and a weakened immune system. Mentally, it can lead to burnout, anxiety, and depression, clouding our judgment and dampening our enthusiasm for life's pleasures and pursuits.

Resentment: The Silent Sufferer

One insidious consequence of always saying yes is the gradual buildup of resentment. This resentment can fester within us, directed towards those who seem to constantly demand our time and energy, and even towards ourselves for not standing firm. It poisons relationships, turning once joyful interactions into sources of stress and discomfort. The irony is palpable; in our desire to be indispensable and liked, we risk harming the very connections we sought to strengthen.

Loss of Self

Constantly prioritizing others' needs and desires over our own leads to a profound loss of self. This loss is not just about neglecting personal hobbies or rest but extends to a diminished sense of autonomy and self-worth. When we fail to set boundaries, we send ourselves the message that our needs, aspirations, and feelings are secondary, if not irrelevant. This can erode our self-esteem and leave us feeling disconnected from our own lives, as though we are spectators rather than active participants.

The Illusion of Being Indispensable

A key driver behind the compulsion to always say yes is the belief in our indispensability—the notion that without our constant contribution, everything will fall apart. This belief is not only false but also harmful. It places undue pressure on us and underestimates the capabilities and resilience of those around us. By learning to say no, we not only allow ourselves the space to breathe and grow but also empower others to step up, share responsibilities, and develop their own strengths.

Navigating the Expectation Trap

Society, and often our immediate circles, can have explicit or implicit expectations of our roles and how we should fulfill them. Women, in particular, are frequently caught in this expectation trap, where the societal blueprint of being nurturing and accommodating conflicts with the personal need for autonomy and self-care. Navigating this trap requires a delicate balance of assertiveness, communication, and self-compassion, challenging as it may be in the face of deeply ingrained societal norms.

The Path to Empowerment

Recognizing the cost of always saying yes is the first step towards empowerment. It is a realization that while we cannot control the requests or demands of others, we have the power to control our responses. This empowerment comes from understanding that saying no is not a rejection of the person or opportunity but a necessary affirmation of our own worth and limits.

Setting boundaries, therefore, is not a selfish act but a profound gesture of self-respect and care. It signals to ourselves and to others that while we are committed to our relationships and responsibilities, we are equally committed to our health, well-being, and personal growth.

Conclusion

The cost of always saying yes is a complex interplay of physical exhaustion, emotional turmoil, and the erosion of self-identity. This chapter has shed light on these costs, not to vilify the act of saying yes, but to highlight the importance of discernment and balance. As we continue through this book, we will explore how to reclaim our power through the art of saying no—how to draw boundaries that protect our well-being, enrich our relationships, and empower us to live more authentically and fully. The journey of setting boundaries is a path to rediscovering our voice and our value, reminding us that we are, indeed, worthy of our own time and care.

Chapter 3:
The Power of No

In the symphony of life, where each yes contributes a note to the melody of our days, the power of saying no holds the potential to harmonize our existence. This chapter delves into the transformative impact of embracing 'no,' a simple yet potent declaration that can reshape our relationships, fortify our sense of self, and catalyze personal and professional growth. Here, we explore the benefits of saying no, the societal reactions to assertive women, and strategies to wield this power with grace and confidence.

Embracing No as an Act of Self-Respect
The act of saying no is, at its core, an affirmation of self-respect. It signals a profound understanding of our worth, needs, and limitations. By declining requests that overextend us or compromise our values, we honor our integrity and prioritize our well-being. This self-respect fosters a healthier relationship with ourselves, laying the foundation for authentic living and decision-making aligned with our true priorities.

The Liberating Effects of No

Saying no has a liberating effect, freeing us from the weight of unnecessary commitments and the pressure of living up to unrealistic expectations. This liberation opens up space in our lives—space for creativity, rest, and activities that bring us joy and fulfillment. It allows us to allocate our time and energy more purposefully, enhancing our productivity and the quality of our engagements. The freedom to choose how we spend our resources is empowering, enabling us to lead lives that are both balanced and meaningful.

No and Relationship Dynamics

Far from alienating us from others, a well-communicated no can enhance our relationships. It sets clear expectations and boundaries, preventing misunderstandings and resentment. By expressing our limits, we invite others to understand and respect our needs, fostering deeper connections based on mutual respect. Moreover, saying no can serve as a model for healthy communication, encouraging others to express their own boundaries and needs.

The Societal Backlash Against Assertive Women

Despite the personal benefits of saying no, women often face societal backlash when they assert their boundaries. Labels such as "difficult," "selfish," or "cold" are not uncommon, reflecting deep-seated stereotypes about gender roles and expectations. This backlash is a testament to the pervasive discomfort with women who prioritize their own needs and challenge the status quo.

Navigating these societal reactions requires resilience and a steadfast belief in one's right to self-determination. It involves challenging internalized messages about female passivity and nurturing and replacing them with a narrative of empowerment and self-care.

Strategies for Saying No with Confidence

Saying no with confidence is an art that can be cultivated through practice and reflection. Here are strategies to help navigate the process:

- **Clarify Your Priorities:** Understanding what truly matters to you makes it easier to identify what warrants a yes and what deserves a no. Keep your priorities in mind as a guiding principle for your decisions.
- **Practice Assertive Communication:** Express your refusal in a firm, clear, and respectful manner. Use "I" statements to take ownership of your decision, such as "I cannot commit to this as I have prioritized other projects."
- **Offer Alternatives When Possible:** If you wish to maintain a relationship or offer support in a different way, suggest alternatives that align with your boundaries, such as referring someone else or proposing a later time.
- **Prepare for Pushback:** Not everyone will respect your no initially. Prepare yourself mentally for potential pushback and rehearse your response to remain firm in your decision.
- **Reflect on Your Feelings:** Pay attention to how saying no affects you emotionally. Recognize any feelings of

guilt or anxiety as normal reactions that will diminish with practice and self-compassion.

The Ripple Effects of No

The decision to say no has ripple effects beyond our immediate personal and professional lives. It challenges societal norms, advocating for a culture where boundaries are respected and self-care is prioritized. Each no is a step toward a more equitable and understanding world, where individuals are valued not for their compliance but for their authenticity and integrity.

Conclusion

The power of no is transformative, with the potential to fundamentally alter how we interact with the world around us. It is a tool for empowerment, self-respect, and liberation, enabling us to lead lives that are not only more balanced and fulfilling but also more aligned with our true selves. As we move forward, let us wield this power with confidence, mindful of the positive changes it can bring about in our lives and the lives of those around us. Saying no is not just a rejection of a request; it is an affirmation of our worth and our right to choose.

Chapter 4:
Identifying Your Boundaries

The journey towards empowerment through boundaries begins with a crucial step: identifying your personal and professional limits. This process is deeply introspective, requiring a candid assessment of your values, needs, and the lines you are unwilling to cross. It's about understanding not just where you stand, but why you stand there. This chapter guides you through the discovery of your boundaries, offering insights and exercises to help you articulate and embrace them.

The Significance of Self-Awareness

Identifying your boundaries is intrinsically tied to self-awareness. It's about knowing who you are at your core, your non-negotiables in life, and what you value most deeply. This understanding serves as a compass, guiding your decisions and interactions. It involves recognizing your emotional responses, understanding your physical and mental limits, and acknowledging your worth.

Recognizing When a Boundary Is Being Crossed

Often, we become aware of our boundaries only when they are being challenged or violated. This recognition can manifest in various ways: discomfort, resentment, anger, or even physical symptoms like tension and fatigue. Paying attention to these signals is crucial; they are your body and mind's way of alerting you to a boundary infringement. Reflecting on these experiences provides valuable insights into where your boundaries lie.

Exercises for Identifying Boundaries

- **Reflect on Past Experiences:** Think about times you felt overwhelmed, disrespected, or uncomfortable. What were the circumstances? These situations often highlight areas where boundaries are needed.
- **Define Your Values:** Write down your top five values. For each, consider what boundaries could protect and express these values in your life.
- **The Ideal Day Exercise:** Imagine your perfect day from start to finish. What does this reveal about your priorities

and limits in terms of time, energy, and engagement with others?

Boundaries in Different Areas of Life

It's important to recognize that boundaries are not one-size-fits-all; they vary significantly across different areas of your life:

- **Emotional Boundaries:** Protect your emotional well-being by regulating who and what you allow to affect your feelings and mood.
- **Physical Boundaries:** Involve your personal space and physical touch. Define what is acceptable and what makes you uncomfortable.
- **Time Boundaries:** Concern how you allocate your time between work, personal life, hobbies, and rest.
- **Intellectual Boundaries:** Relate to your thoughts, beliefs, and values. They involve respecting differing viewpoints while asserting your own.
- **Digital Boundaries:** Govern your engagement with technology and social media, including what you share and how you interact online.

Communicating Your Boundaries

Once identified, the next step is learning how to effectively communicate your boundaries. It's about expressing your limits clearly, calmly, and without apology. This communication is not a one-time event but an ongoing conversation as your needs and relationships evolve.

Strategies for Boundary Setting

- **Start Small:** Begin with boundaries that are easier to enforce and communicate. This builds confidence and sets a precedent for more significant boundaries later.
- **Use "I" Statements:** Make your boundaries about your needs and feelings ("I feel overwhelmed when I take on extra tasks") rather than blaming the other person.
- **Be Direct but Kind:** Clarity is key in boundary setting. Avoid ambiguity, but deliver your message with empathy and respect.
- **Practice, Practice, Practice:** Like any skill, effectively setting boundaries takes practice. Role-play with a trusted friend or in front of a mirror to build your confidence.

Dealing with Boundary Pushback

It's natural to encounter resistance when you start setting boundaries, especially if it's new to you and those around you. The key is to remain firm yet understanding. Reiterate your boundary if necessary, and don't be afraid to disengage from situations where your boundaries are not respected.

Conclusion

Identifying and setting boundaries is an act of self-love and respect. It's about acknowledging your worth, understanding your needs, and taking control of your life. This chapter has laid the groundwork for recognizing and establishing your boundaries. As you move forward, remember that boundaries are not barriers to connection but the foundation upon which healthy, fulfilling relationships are built. By honoring your boundaries, you invite others to understand and respect your needs, creating a space for mutual respect and genuine connection.

Chapter 5: Communicating Your Boundaries

After identifying your boundaries, the next step—and perhaps one of the most challenging—is communicating them effectively. This chapter is dedicated to navigating the intricacies of boundary communication, offering tools and strategies to express your limits with clarity and confidence, all while maintaining respect and empathy in your relationships.

The Art of Assertive Communication

Assertive communication is key to expressing your boundaries. It strikes a balance between passive submission and aggressive confrontation, allowing you to state your needs and limits clearly without infringing on the rights of others. This communication style is characterized by openness, honesty, and directness, and it is fundamental in setting and maintaining healthy boundaries.

Preparing to Communicate

Before you approach a boundary conversation, preparation is crucial. This involves understanding your boundary deeply— why it's important to you and the consequences of it being disregarded. Reflect on potential responses and have a clear idea of what you're willing to compromise on, if anything, and what is non-negotiable.

Effective Strategies for Communicating Boundaries

- **Be Clear and Specific:** Ambiguity is the enemy of effective boundary setting. Be as clear as possible about what you are requesting or refusing. For example, rather than saying, "I need more space," specify, "I need the evenings to myself from 7 to 9 PM."
- **Use "I" Statements:** This technique focuses the conversation on your feelings and needs rather than on blaming or criticizing the other person. For example, "I feel overwhelmed when I don't have time to myself in the evenings."
- **Practice Empathy:** Acknowledge the other person's feelings and perspectives. This does not mean compromising your boundary but showing that you respect and understand their position.
- **Rehearse Your Message:** If you anticipate that setting a boundary might be difficult, practice what you want to say ahead of time. This can help you stay focused and calm during the actual conversation.
- **Timing is Key:** Choose a time to communicate your boundary when both you and the other person are calm and not preoccupied with other stressful issues.

Dealing with Pushback

When you start setting boundaries, especially with people who are used to you saying yes, pushback is inevitable. It can range from mild surprise to outright resistance. Here's how to handle it:

- **Stay Firm but Kind:** Reiterate your boundary clearly. You might need to repeat yourself several times before the message is fully understood and accepted.
- **Avoid Justifying or Over-Explaining:** While it's essential to explain your boundary, avoid falling into the trap of over-justification, which can lead to unnecessary arguments.
- **Offer Alternatives:** If possible, suggest alternatives that respect your boundaries but still consider the other person's needs.
- **Prepare for Emotional Responses:** The person you're setting boundaries with may feel hurt or disappointed. Prepare for this, and reaffirm your commitment to the relationship despite the boundary.

The Role of Non-Verbal Communication

Non-verbal cues play a significant role in how your message is received. Maintain open body language, make eye contact, and ensure your tone of voice reflects your message's seriousness. These signals can reinforce the importance of your boundary.

Boundary Conversations in Different Contexts

The way you communicate your boundaries may vary depending on the context and your relationship with the other person. Whether it's in personal relationships, at work, or online, tailor your approach to suit the situation while maintaining the core principles of clear, assertive communication.

Building a Culture of Respect

By effectively communicating your boundaries, you contribute to a culture of mutual respect and understanding. It encourages others to express their limits, fostering healthier and more balanced relationships. Remember, setting boundaries is not just about protecting your well-being; it's about building relationships where everyone feels valued and heard.

Conclusion

Communicating your boundaries is an ongoing process, one that requires patience, practice, and resilience. It's about finding your voice and using it to advocate for your needs and well-being. As you become more skilled in expressing your boundaries, you'll find that your relationships become more genuine, your stress levels decrease, and your self-respect deepens. This chapter has equipped you with the tools to start this journey, encouraging you to step into your power and communicate your boundaries with confidence and grace.

Chapter 6:
Setting Boundaries in Personal Relationships

Navigating personal relationships with clear boundaries is crucial for maintaining healthy connections and ensuring personal well-being. Whether it's with family, friends, or romantic partners, the art of setting boundaries can significantly impact the quality and sustainability of these relationships. This chapter explores strategies for setting boundaries in personal relationships, offering insights on balancing respect for others with respect for oneself.

Understanding the Need for Boundaries in Relationships

Boundaries in personal relationships help define where one person ends and another begins. They allow individuals to express their needs, desires, and limits, fostering a sense of mutual respect and understanding. Without clear boundaries, relationships can become sources of stress, resentment, and conflict, leading to emotional exhaustion and even relationship breakdown.

Identifying Boundaries with Partners, Family, and Friends

Each type of relationship presents unique challenges and opportunities for boundary setting. With romantic partners, boundaries might relate to communication, personal space, or financial independence. In family relationships, boundaries might concern expectations around time, support, or involvement in personal decisions. With friends, boundaries may involve balancing availability for support with the need for personal time.

Communicating Boundaries Effectively

The key to setting boundaries in personal relationships is effective communication. Here are steps to guide the conversation:

- **Choose the Right Moment:** Initiate the conversation when both parties are calm and unlikely to be distracted or defensive.

- **Express Your Feelings and Needs:** Use "I" statements to convey how certain behaviors affect you and what you need moving forward.
- **Be Specific and Clear:** Clearly define what is acceptable and what is not. Avoid vague statements that can lead to misunderstandings.
- **Listen Actively:** Be prepared to listen to the other person's perspective and feelings. Boundary setting is a two-way conversation.
- **Be Prepared for Resistance:** Change can be challenging. Remain firm in your boundaries while showing empathy and understanding.

Balancing Flexibility and Firmness

While it's important to be clear and firm in your boundaries, flexibility is also crucial. Life is unpredictable, and circumstances change. Be open to revisiting and adjusting boundaries as needed, ensuring they continue to serve everyone's best interests.

Case Studies: Navigating Common Scenarios

- **Scenario 1: Overbearing Family Members:** Learn how to assert your independence while maintaining loving relationships, especially during life transitions like marriage or career changes.
- **Scenario 2: Clingy or Demanding Friends:** Strategies for managing friendships that drain your energy or infringe on your personal time without alienating those you care about.

- **Scenario 3: Partners with Different Needs for Space:** Balancing the need for closeness with the need for individuality in romantic relationships.

The Role of Self-Care in Setting Boundaries

Setting boundaries is an act of self-care. It requires recognizing your worth and prioritizing your mental, emotional, and physical health. Remember, setting boundaries not only benefits you but also teaches others how to treat you with respect and consideration.

Dealing with Guilt and Anxiety

It's common to feel guilty or anxious when setting boundaries, especially if you're not used to prioritizing your own needs. These feelings often stem from fear of conflict or upsetting others. Acknowledge these feelings, understand they're a natural part of the process, and remind yourself of the importance of your boundaries for your well-being.

Maintaining Boundaries Over Time

Setting boundaries is not a one-time event but an ongoing practice. It involves regular reflection, communication, and adjustment as relationships evolve. Consistency in maintaining your boundaries reinforces their importance to both yourself and others.

Conclusion

Setting boundaries in personal relationships is essential for fostering healthy, respectful, and fulfilling connections. It allows for personal growth, mutual respect, and the development of stronger, more authentic relationships. By understanding the need for boundaries, communicating them effectively, and balancing flexibility with firmness, you can navigate the complexities of personal relationships with confidence and grace. Remember, the quality of your relationships significantly impacts your overall happiness and well-being, making boundary setting not just a personal priority but a necessity.

Chapter 7:
Setting Boundaries at Work

The workplace is a complex network of relationships, expectations, and demands. Navigating this environment requires clear boundaries to maintain professional integrity, personal well-being, and work-life balance. This chapter explores the significance of setting boundaries at work and offers strategies to assert them effectively, fostering a healthy and productive professional life.

The Importance of Professional Boundaries

Professional boundaries protect your mental health, prevent burnout, and contribute to a positive work environment. They help manage workload, interpersonal relationships, and personal space, ensuring you can perform at your best without compromising your well-being.

Identifying Your Work Boundaries

Start by identifying what you need to work effectively while maintaining your well-being. Consider aspects such as work hours, communication preferences, task delegation, and personal space. Recognize the difference between being flexible and being overextended. Reflect on past experiences where you felt overwhelmed or undervalued, and use these insights to define your boundaries.

Communicating Boundaries Clearly

Effective communication is key to establishing work boundaries. Here are some strategies:

- **Be Proactive:** Address potential boundary issues before they become problematic. Setting expectations early can prevent misunderstandings.
- **Use Clear, Assertive Language:** Express your needs and limitations confidently. For example, "I can complete this task by end-of-day Thursday, rather than Wednesday, to ensure it meets our quality standards."
- **Seek Solutions:** When discussing boundaries, focus on finding solutions that align with your needs and the organization's goals. This collaborative approach demonstrates your commitment to your work and respect for team dynamics.

Navigating Workloads and Delegation

One of the most challenging aspects of workplace boundaries involves managing workloads and delegation. Learn to say no to additional tasks when your plate is already full, and delegate tasks appropriately. This requires understanding your priorities and communicating them effectively to your team and superiors.

Case Studies: Navigating Work Boundaries

- **Scenario 1: The Always-On Culture:** Strategies for setting boundaries around work hours and availability in a culture that expects constant connectivity.
- **Scenario 2: Handling Overbearing Colleagues:** How to assert your professional space and manage relationships with colleagues who overstep boundaries.
- **Scenario 3: Negotiating Workloads:** Techniques for discussing workload management with superiors, including how to say no or request extensions.

Maintaining Boundaries in a Remote Work Environment

Remote work presents unique challenges for boundary setting. The blending of home and workspaces can erode the distinction between personal and professional time. Establishing physical and temporal boundaries is crucial. Define a dedicated workspace, set clear work hours, and communicate your availability to your team.

The Role of Leadership in Respecting Boundaries

Leaders play a critical role in setting the tone for boundary respect within the workplace. Encourage open dialogue about boundaries, model respectful behavior, and address boundary violations promptly. A leadership approach that values employee well-being sets a positive example and contributes to a supportive work culture.

Dealing with Boundary Violations

Despite clear communication, boundary violations may occur. Address these situations promptly and directly. Reiterate your boundaries, explain the impact of the violation, and discuss steps to prevent future occurrences. Seek support from HR or management if needed.

Strategies for Work-Life Balance

Maintaining work-life balance is an ongoing process that requires vigilance and adjustment. Regularly assess your work habits, commitments outside work, and overall well-being. Be prepared to renegotiate boundaries as your personal and professional circumstances evolve.

Conclusion

Setting boundaries at work is not just about saying no; it's about creating a sustainable work environment that respects your needs and those of your colleagues. It requires clarity, communication, and the courage to uphold your principles in the face of pressure. By establishing and maintaining clear professional boundaries, you safeguard your well-being, enhance your productivity, and contribute to a positive and respectful workplace culture. Remember, boundaries are a sign of professionalism and self-respect, key components of success and satisfaction in your career.

Chapter 8:
Digital Boundaries

In today's interconnected world, our digital lives have become an extension of our physical existence, blurring the lines between public and private, work and leisure. The constant barrage of notifications, emails, and social media updates demands our attention, often at the expense of our mental well-being. Setting digital boundaries is crucial for maintaining balance, protecting our privacy, and nurturing our real-life relationships. This chapter explores the importance of establishing digital boundaries and provides strategies for managing our online presence and technology use.

The Need for Digital Boundaries

The digital realm offers unparalleled opportunities for connection, learning, and entertainment. However, without clear boundaries, it can lead to information overload, privacy concerns, and a disconnect from physical experiences and relationships. Digital boundaries help us navigate the online world responsibly, ensuring that technology serves us, not the other way around.

Identifying Your Digital Boundaries

Start by assessing your digital habits and their impact on your life. Consider questions like: How much time do I spend online? Does social media use affect my mood? Am I comfortable with the privacy settings on my digital accounts? Use your answers to identify areas where you need to set or reinforce boundaries.

Strategies for Managing Social Media and Technology Use

- **Limit Screen Time:** Set specific times of the day for checking emails, social media, and other non-essential digital activities. Use app timers or screen time tracking features to hold yourself accountable.

- **Curate Your Digital Environment:** Unfollow accounts that trigger negative emotions or waste your time. Prioritize content that adds value to your life, whether it's educational, inspirational, or simply brings you joy.

- **Protect Your Privacy:** Regularly review the privacy settings on your social media accounts and digital devices. Be mindful of the information you share online and who has access to it.

- **Digital Detox:** Allocate time each week to disconnect from digital devices and engage in offline activities. This can help reset your digital habits and reduce dependency on technology.

- **Mindful Consumption:** Be selective about the digital content you consume. Ask yourself whether it enriches your life or contributes to feelings of inadequacy or anxiety.

Navigating Digital Communication

Digital communication, while convenient, can lead to misunderstandings and conflict due to the absence of non-verbal cues. Establish boundaries around digital communication by preferring face-to-face or voice conversations for important discussions. Be clear and respectful in your online interactions, and avoid engaging in digital communication when emotions are high.

Case Studies: Setting Digital Boundaries

- **Scenario 1: The Always-Connected Employee:** Learn strategies for setting boundaries around work communication outside of office hours, including how to communicate these boundaries to your employer.
- **Scenario 2: Social Media Overuse:** Explore techniques for reducing social media consumption and mitigating its impact on your mental health and real-life relationships.
- **Scenario 3: Online Harassment:** Understand the steps to take if you experience harassment online, including how to report abuse and protect your mental well-being.

The Impact of Digital Boundaries on Relationships

Setting digital boundaries can positively impact your relationships by ensuring that technology use does not overshadow face-to-face interactions. Discuss digital boundaries with your partner, family, and friends to foster understanding and respect for each other's digital space and preferences.

The Challenge of Enforcing Digital Boundaries

Enforcing digital boundaries requires discipline and consistency. Expect setbacks, but view them as opportunities to reassess and strengthen your boundaries. Support from friends and family can be invaluable in maintaining these boundaries.

Conclusion

Establishing digital boundaries is essential for navigating the complexities of the digital age with our well-being intact. It allows us to reap the benefits of technology without letting it dominate our lives. By being intentional about our digital habits, protecting our privacy, and prioritizing real-life connections, we can maintain a healthy balance between our online and offline worlds. Remember, the power to control your digital life lies in your hands—use it wisely to create a fulfilling and balanced existence.

Chapter 9:
The Self-Care Connection

Setting boundaries is not just a practice of defining limits with others; it's a profound act of self-care. This chapter delves into how establishing boundaries is integral to nurturing your mental, emotional, and physical well-being. It offers insights into the symbiotic relationship between self-care and boundaries, illustrating how one reinforces the other, creating a foundation for a life lived with intention and respect for oneself.

Boundaries as Self-Care

Self-care often conjures images of indulgent activities or routines aimed at relaxation and stress relief. While these practices are beneficial, at its core, self-care is about making choices that prioritize your well-being and respect your needs. Setting boundaries is a paramount form of self-care because it involves acknowledging your limits and ensuring you are not spread too thin, physically or emotionally. It's about giving yourself permission to say no, to rest, and to prioritize activities that replenish rather than deplete you.

Understanding the Connection

The connection between self-care and boundaries lies in the recognition of one's worth and the active decision to honor that worth through actions. By setting boundaries, you assert that your time, energy, and emotional well-being are valuable. This assertion not only communicates to others how you expect to be treated but also reinforces your self-esteem and self-respect.

Building Routines Around Boundaries

Incorporating boundaries into your self-care routine involves both setting limits on what you will tolerate from others and creating space for activities that nurture you. This might look like:

- **Time Boundaries:** Allocating specific times for work, leisure, and self-care activities, ensuring each aspect of your life receives attention without overwhelming you.
- **Emotional Boundaries:** Choosing to engage in relationships and activities that support your emotional health, and distancing yourself from toxic influences.

- **Physical Boundaries:** Listening to your body's needs, whether it's for rest, movement, or nourishment, and respecting those needs through your actions.

The Role of Self-Compassion and Self-Respect

At the heart of boundary setting for self-care is self-compassion and self-respect. These qualities allow you to forgive yourself when you falter, to treat yourself with kindness, and to steadfastly believe in your right to care for yourself. They remind you that self-care is not selfish but essential for sustaining your ability to care for others and engage with the world.

Overcoming Obstacles to Self-Care

Setting boundaries for self-care can be challenging, particularly when faced with guilt, fear of rejection, or internalized beliefs about selfishness. Overcoming these obstacles involves:

- **Reframing Self-Care:** Understanding self-care as a necessity rather than a luxury or an act of selfishness.
- **Practicing Assertiveness:** Building the skill to communicate your needs and boundaries confidently and respectfully.
- **Seeking Support:** Surrounding yourself with a supportive community that respects your boundaries and encourages your self-care efforts.

Cultivating a Self-Care Mindset

Adopting a self-care mindset means recognizing that taking care of yourself is not a one-time activity but a continuous practice. It involves making daily choices that reflect your commitment to your well-being and adjusting your boundaries as your needs and circumstances evolve.

Case Studies: Integrating Boundaries into Self-Care

- **Scenario 1: The Overcommitted Volunteer:** Strategies for balancing the desire to help with the need for personal time and how to gracefully decline additional commitments.
- **Scenario 2: Navigating Family Expectations:** Techniques for managing family demands while prioritizing self-care, including how to communicate your needs during family gatherings.
- **Scenario 3: The Burnt-Out Employee:** Approaches to asserting work-life balance, managing workplace stress, and carving out time for relaxation and hobbies.

Conclusion

The self-care connection to setting boundaries is undeniable and essential. By honoring your limits and respecting your needs, you foster a life of balance, well-being, and fulfillment. This chapter has underscored the importance of viewing boundaries as a critical component of self-care, offering practical strategies for integrating them into your life. Remember, the act of setting boundaries is not just about saying no to others but about saying yes to yourself, affirming your worth, and nurturing your overall health. Embrace this practice with kindness and compassion, and watch as your life transforms into one of deeper contentment and resilience.

Chapter 10:
Overcoming Challenges

While the journey toward setting and maintaining boundaries is enriching and empowering, it is not without its challenges. Encountering resistance, navigating feelings of guilt, and the ongoing need for adjustment are all part of the process. This chapter addresses these common obstacles, offering insights and strategies to overcome them, ensuring that your boundaries strengthen rather than weaken over time.

Recognizing Common Obstacles

The path to effective boundary setting is often met with external and internal obstacles. Externally, resistance can come from those accustomed to your previous boundary-less state. Internally, feelings of guilt, fear of rejection, or worry about hurting others can undermine your resolve. Recognizing these obstacles as normal and common is the first step toward overcoming them.

Maintaining Boundaries Against Pushback

Resistance from others can manifest as guilt-tripping, anger, or even manipulation. Overcoming this pushback requires a firm yet compassionate approach:

- **Reaffirm Your Boundaries:** Clearly restate your limits, emphasizing their importance for your well-being.
- **Stay Consistent:** Consistency reinforces the seriousness of your boundaries. Changes in behavior take time; perseverance is key.

- **Seek Support:** Having a support system can bolster your confidence and provide perspective when facing resistance.

Dealing with Internal Conflict

Feelings of guilt or fear are often the most significant barriers to maintaining boundaries. To navigate these feelings:

- **Reflect on the Source:** Understanding why you feel guilty can help address the underlying beliefs fueling these emotions.

- **Practice Self-Compassion:** Remind yourself that setting boundaries is an act of self-respect and necessary for your health and happiness.

- **Visualize Positive Outcomes:** Focus on the benefits of boundary setting, such as increased energy, peace, and improved relationships.

The Art of Flexible Boundaries

While boundaries should be firm, they also need to be flexible to accommodate life's changing circumstances. Being too rigid can strain relationships and create unnecessary stress. Flexibility involves:

- **Assessing Situations Individually:** Consider the context and whether adjusting a boundary could lead to a mutually beneficial outcome.

- **Communicating Changes:** If a boundary shifts, communicate this change clearly to prevent confusion.

- **Reevaluating Regularly:** Life changes, and so do our needs. Regularly assess your boundaries to ensure they still serve you well.

Reinforcing Boundaries Over Time

Boundary setting is an ongoing process. To reinforce your boundaries:

- **Regular Check-ins:** Periodically review your boundaries to ensure they align with your current needs and values.
- **Celebrate Successes:** Acknowledge when a boundary has protected your well-being or improved a relationship. Celebrating these victories can motivate you to maintain your boundaries.
- **Adjust as Necessary:** Be open to adjusting your boundaries as your relationships and circumstances evolve.

Case Studies: Navigating Boundary Challenges

- **Scenario 1: The Persistent Family Member:** Tactics for dealing with family who refuse to accept new boundaries, focusing on consistency and the importance of support.
- **Scenario 2: The Guilt-Inducing Friend:** Strategies for overcoming internal guilt when setting boundaries with friends who do not understand or respect your limits.
- **Scenario 3: The Workplace Without Boundaries:** Approaches to reinforcing boundaries in a challenging

work environment, including seeking allies and when to escalate concerns.

Conclusion

Setting and maintaining boundaries is a dynamic and challenging journey. It requires courage, consistency, and a deep commitment to your own well-being. While obstacles are inevitable, they are not insurmountable. Each challenge presents an opportunity for growth, self-discovery, and deeper connection with yourself and others. By embracing flexibility, practicing self-compassion, and seeking support, you can navigate these challenges successfully, reinforcing your boundaries and enriching your life. Remember, boundaries are not barriers but bridges to a more authentic, empowered, and fulfilled self.

Conclusion:
Embracing a Boundary-Minded Life

As we close the final chapter of "Permission to Say No: Empowering Yourself through Boundaries," we reflect on the journey we've embarked upon together. Setting boundaries is more than a mere act of self-preservation; it's a declaration of self-worth and a commitment to living authentically. Through the pages of this book, we've explored the multifaceted landscape of boundaries—from understanding their importance to communicating them effectively, and navigating the challenges they present in our personal and professional lives.

The Transformative Power of Boundaries

Boundaries are transformative. They reshape our relationships, our work, and most importantly, our relationship with ourselves. They teach us that saying no is not an act of rejection but a profound affirmation of our values, needs, and well-being. This book has aimed to guide you in discovering your boundaries, asserting them with confidence, and embracing the freedom and respect they bring to your life.

The Journey Is Ongoing

The journey toward a boundary-minded life does not end with the last page of this book. It is an ongoing process of self-discovery, trial, and adjustment. As you grow and evolve, so too will your boundaries. They will be tested, and at times, they may falter. But with each challenge, you'll gain deeper insight into your needs and how to protect them. Remember, setting boundaries is not a one-time task but a continuous practice—a practice that requires patience, courage, and self-compassion.

Challenges Are Opportunities

The challenges you'll face in setting and maintaining boundaries are not roadblocks but opportunities for growth. They will teach you about your strengths, your vulnerabilities, and the depth of your resolve. Facing resistance from others, dealing with internal guilt, and adjusting boundaries in response to life's changes are all part of the journey. These experiences will strengthen your ability to advocate for yourself and foster relationships based on mutual respect and understanding.

Building a Supportive Community

One of the most valuable aspects of setting boundaries is the community you build along the way. Seeking support from friends, family, or professionals who respect and encourage your boundary-setting efforts can provide strength and validation. Surround yourself with people who understand the importance of boundaries, and don't be afraid to distance yourself from those who consistently disregard them. A supportive community is a cornerstone of a boundary-minded life.

Embracing Flexibility and Forgiveness

Flexibility and forgiveness are key components of successfully living with boundaries. Be open to reevaluating and adjusting your boundaries as your life and relationships evolve. Forgive yourself when things don't go as planned or when you struggle to maintain a boundary. Self-compassion is a crucial ally in your journey, reminding you that perfection is not the goal—authenticity and well-being are.

The Ripple Effect of Boundaries

The impact of setting boundaries extends far beyond your immediate environment. By prioritizing your well-being and respecting your limits, you model healthy behavior for those around you. You contribute to a culture where boundaries are understood, respected, and valued—a culture that recognizes the dignity and worth of every individual.

A Final Reflection

As you move forward, remember that the permission to say no is not something you need to earn; it is your inherent right. Your needs, feelings, and well-being are valid and deserving of respect. Setting boundaries is an act of courage and an expression of self-love. It is a commitment to living a life that honors your true self, a life filled with purpose, respect, and fulfillment.

Looking Ahead

As you continue on your journey, carry with you the lessons, strategies, and insights you've gained from this book. Remember that each day offers a new opportunity to live more authentically, to set boundaries that reflect your values and needs, and to build a life that truly feels like your own. Embrace the challenges and changes with openness and resilience, knowing that each step, no matter how small, is a step toward a more empowered and boundary-minded you.

In closing, I invite you to view boundary setting not as a task to be completed but as a way of being—a way of living deeply aligned with your true self. May your boundaries bring you closer to the life you aspire to live, filled with joy, peace, and profound self-respect. Here's to embracing a boundary-minded life, one "no" at a time.

About the Author

Garrett Couch is a transformative voice in the realm of personal development, recognized for his insightful approach to self-empowerment and emotional resilience. With a background in psychology and a lifelong passion for helping individuals unlock their full potential, Garrett has dedicated his career to guiding others on the journey to self-discovery and personal growth.

Garrett's writing is inspired by his own experiences and challenges in navigating the complex landscape of interpersonal relationships and self-esteem. His empathetic and practical approach to setting boundaries emerges from years of research, personal practice, and coaching others to find balance and fulfillment in their lives. Garrett's work is rooted in the belief that everyone deserves to live a life marked by dignity, respect, and self-compassion.

As the author of "Permission to Say No: Empowering Yourself through Boundaries," Garrett draws upon his expertise to offer readers a comprehensive guide to reclaiming their space, peace, and autonomy. His teachings transcend simple advice, delving deep into the mechanisms of boundary setting and the transformative power it holds for personal liberation.

Outside of his writing, Garrett is an engaging speaker and dedicated mentor, known for his ability to connect with audiences on a deeply personal level. His workshops and seminars have empowered countless individuals to reshape their lives through the art of boundary setting, earning him a respected place among today's leading self-help experts.

Garrett resides in Louisville, Kentucky, where he continues to explore the depths of human potential and self-care practices. When he's not writing or speaking, he enjoys nature walks, meditation, and the ongoing study of human behavior. Garrett's mission is to inspire a boundary-minded revolution, fostering a world where individuals confidently assert their right to say no, prioritizing their well-being in the pursuit of a more authentic and fulfilling life.